CRANES

by Amanda Doering Tourville
illustrated by Zachary Trover

Content Consultant:
Paul M. Goodrum, PE, PhD, Associate Professor
Department of Civil Engineering, University of Kentucky

magic wagon

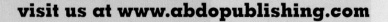

visit us at www.abdopublishing.com

Published by Magic Wagon, a division of the ABDO Group, 8000 West 78th Street, Edina, Minnesota, 55439. Copyright © 2009 by Abdo Consulting Group, Inc. International copyrights reserved in all countries. All rights reserved. No part of this book may be reproduced in any form without written permission from the publisher.

Looking Glass Library™ is a trademark and logo of Magic Wagon.

Printed in the United States.

Text by Amanda Doering Tourville
Illustrations by Zachary Trover
Edited by Patricia Stockland
Cover and interior design by Emily Love

Library of Congress Cataloging-in-Publication Data
Tourville, Amanda Doering, 1980-
 Cranes / by Amanda Doering Tourville ; illustrated by Zachary Trover.
    p. cm. — (Mighty machines)
 Includes index.
 ISBN 978-1-60270-622-4
 1. Cranes, derricks, etc.—Juvenile literature. I. Trover, Zachary, ill. II. Title.
 TJ1363.T7265 2009
 621.8'73—dc22
                                          2008035992

Table of Contents

What Are Cranes?

Cranes are machines that lift and move heavy loads. They help construct buildings, bridges, and roads. They also help load trains and ships.

Cranes get their name from the animal by the same name. Cranes are birds with long necks. One part of the machine looks like the long neck of the bird.

How Are Cranes Used?

Construction workers often use cranes. Cranes help make new buildings, roads, and bridges. They are also used to fix roads and bridges.

Cranes are used at factories and steel mills, too. They lift and move large objects. And, large farms use cranes to lift bales of hay.

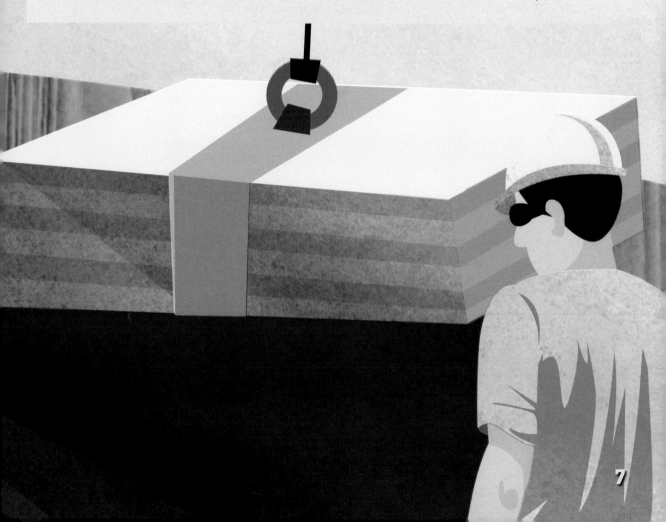

Where Are Cranes Used?

Cranes are used all over the world. They build tall skyscrapers in large cities. And, they help farmers in rural areas. Cranes are used near large bodies of water. They load and unload ships. Cranes are built strong to be used anywhere they are needed.

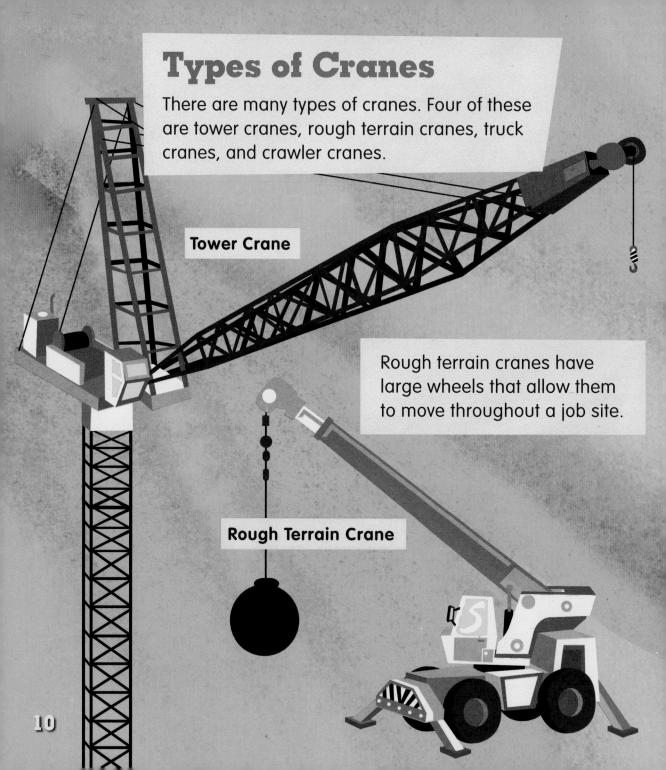

Types of Cranes

There are many types of cranes. Four of these are tower cranes, rough terrain cranes, truck cranes, and crawler cranes.

Tower Crane

Rough terrain cranes have large wheels that allow them to move throughout a job site.

Rough Terrain Crane

Truck cranes are mobile cranes. This means their bases can move. A truck is the base for the truck crane.

Truck Crane

Crawler Crane

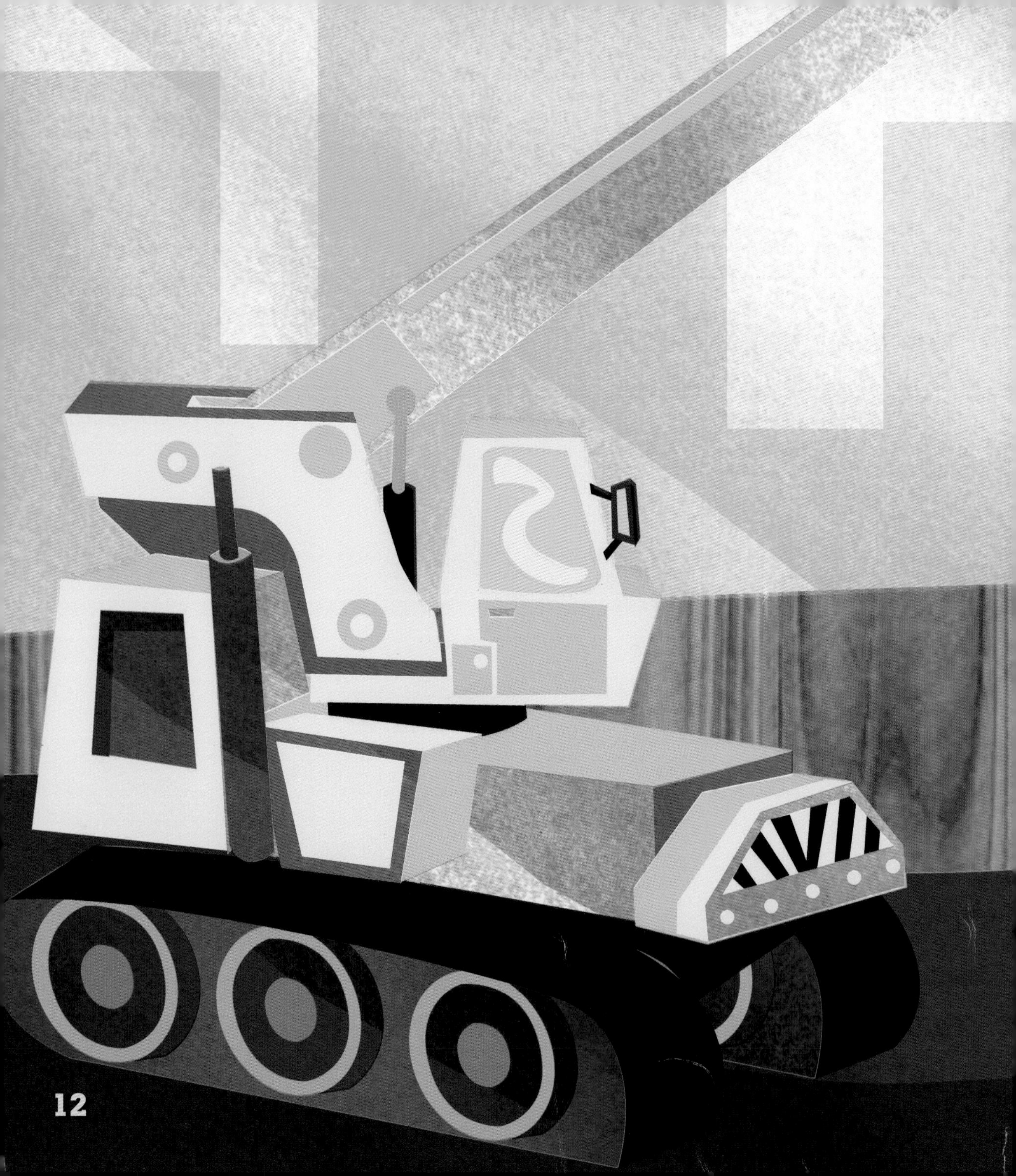

Crawler cranes have tracks instead of tires. The tracks keep the crane from sinking into the soil. The tracks make the crane move much slower. So, large trucks or trains move crawler cranes from site to site.

Tower cranes are built on-site. Sometimes they are built within skyscrapers that they are helping to build. Tower cranes grow taller along with the skyscrapers. The base for a tower crane is bolted into concrete.

16

Parts of Cranes

The long steel arm that lifts the load is called the boom. A crane with a shorter boom can lift a heavier load.

Some cranes have a jib on the end of the boom. The jib extends out to make the arm longer. On a tower crane, the long steel arm is called the jib.

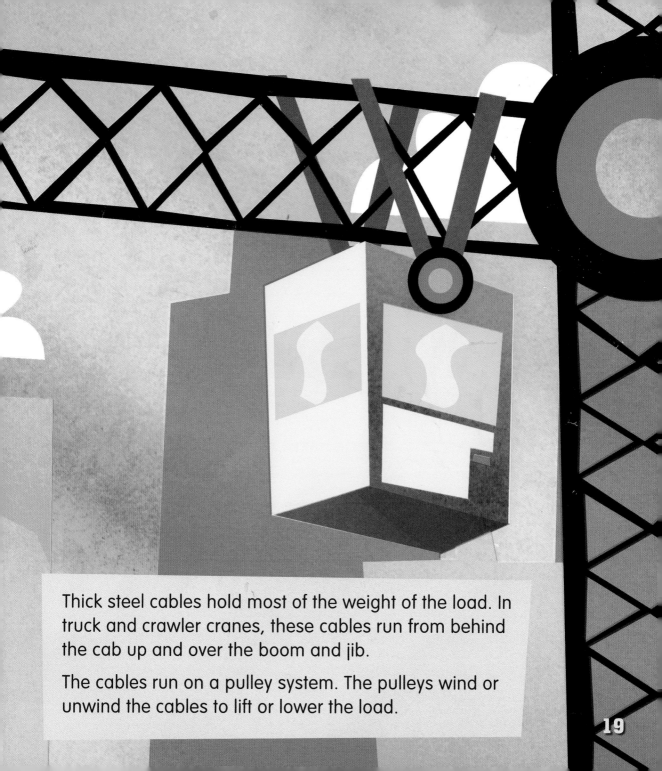

Thick steel cables hold most of the weight of the load. In truck and crawler cranes, these cables run from behind the cab up and over the boom and jib.

The cables run on a pulley system. The pulleys wind or unwind the cables to lift or lower the load.

Most cranes lift their loads with a large hook. It hangs from the steel cables. The hook has a safety latch so the load cannot slide off the hook.

Cranes can be fitted with other attachments to help them do other jobs. An electromagnet can be added to lift metal, such as steel beams. A clamshell bucket can be added so the crane can dig.

Outriggers act like legs to balance cranes while lifting heavy loads. They keep the machines from falling over.

Counterweights are placed on the back of a crane. These keep the crane from falling forward when it lifts heavy loads. Counterweights help to balance the load being lifted.

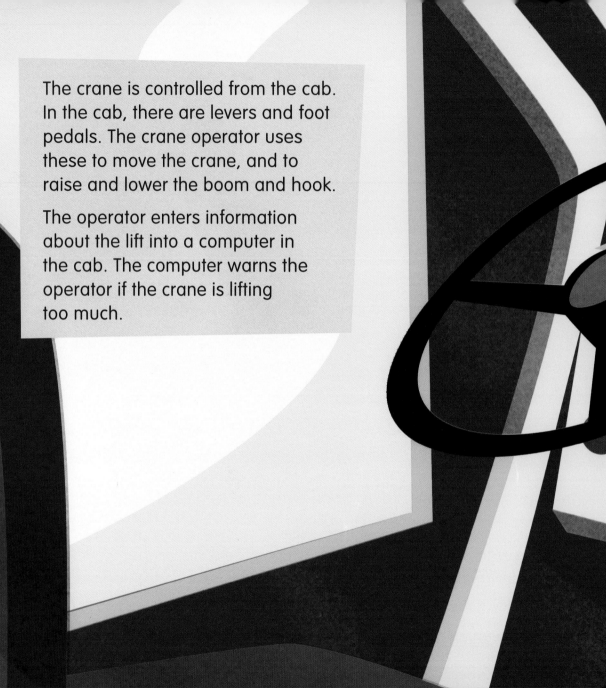

The crane is controlled from the cab. In the cab, there are levers and foot pedals. The crane operator uses these to move the crane, and to raise and lower the boom and hook.

The operator enters information about the lift into a computer in the cab. The computer warns the operator if the crane is lifting too much.

Cranes Are Mighty Machines!

Cranes are important machines. They lift and move enormous loads high into the air. Without cranes, building skyscrapers would be impossible. Cranes use their mighty strength to get the job done.

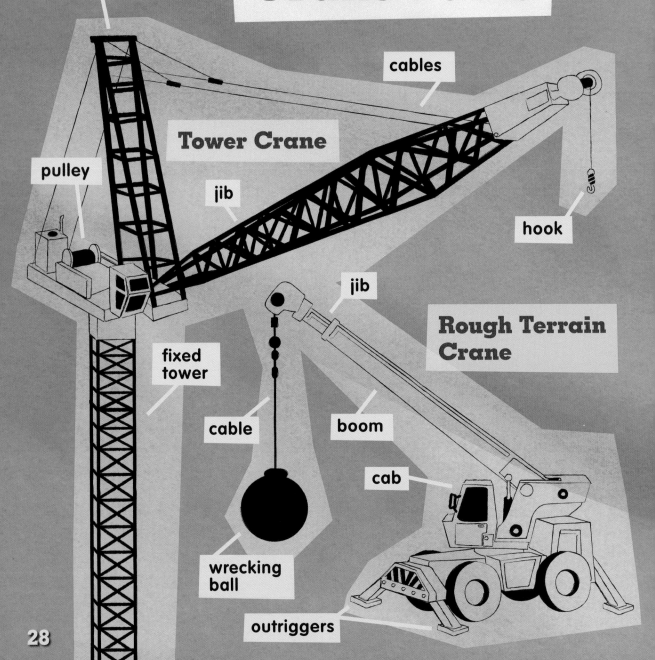

Crane Parts

mast

cables

Tower Crane

pulley

jib

hook

fixed tower

jib

Rough Terrain Crane

cable

boom

cab

wrecking ball

outriggers

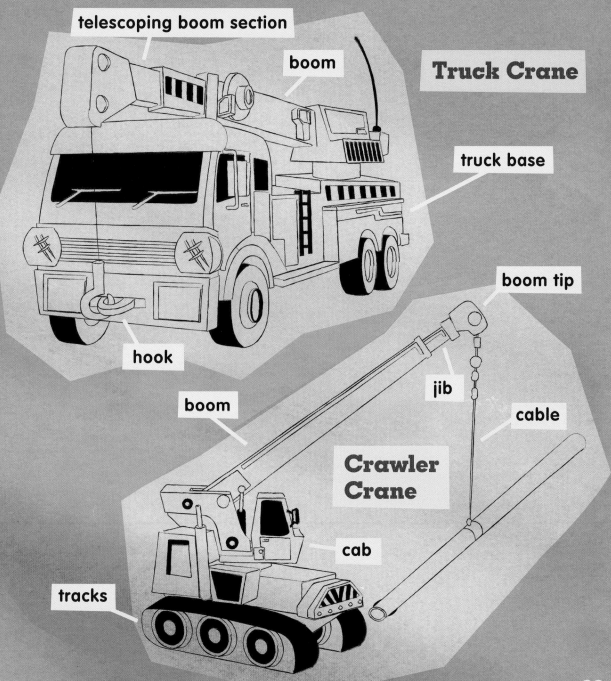

telescoping boom section

boom

Truck Crane

truck base

hook

boom tip

boom

jib

cable

Crawler Crane

cab

tracks

29

Fun Facts

⚙ Truck cranes are the only type of crane that can be driven on the road. They can move from site to site on their own. But truck cranes cannot move while they are lifting a load.

⚙ Sea World uses truck cranes to lift killer whales out of their tanks.

⚙ The crane operator relies on at least three other crew members to perform a lift. The rigger attaches the load to the crane. The oiler makes sure that the crane's parts are all in the proper position. The oiler also makes sure that the load is secure. The signalman uses hand signals to tell the operator how to lift and move the load.

⚙ Mobile cranes, such as truck cranes and crawler cranes, build tower cranes.

⚙ Cranes are very expensive. Many construction firms rent cranes instead of buying them. It costs more than $75,000 to rent a 150-foot-tall (46 m) tower crane for a month.

⚙ If a crane tries to lift a load too high, a set of lights will light up in the cab to let the operator know.

Glossary

cable—a wire rope of great strength.

concrete—a strong building material made out of cement and water.

construction—the act of building or making something.

mobile—able to move or be moved.

pulley—a wheel over which a rope or cable may be pulled to help heavy loads move or change direction.

rural—relating to country life.

Web Sites

To learn more about cranes, visit ABDO Group online at **www.abdopublishing.com**. Web sites about cranes are featured on our Book Links page. These links are routinely monitored and updated to provide the most current information available.

Index